I Wonder Why
The Sea Is Salty

and other questions about the oceans

Anita Ganeri

KINGFISHER

KINGFISHER
Kingfisher Publications Plc,
New Penderel House,
283–288 High Holborn,
London WC1V 7HZ
www.kingfisherpub.com

First published by Kingfisher Publications Plc 1995
First published in this format 2002
1 0 9 8 7 6 5
TS/1104/SHA/*UP UNV/126.6MA/F

Copyright © Kingfisher Publications Plc 1995

A CIP catalogue record for this book is available from
the British Library

ISBN 0 7534 0751 5

Printed in Taiwan

Series editor: Jackie Gaff
Series designer: David West Children's Books
Author: Anita Ganeri
Consultant: Michael Chinery, Keith Lye
Editors: Claire Llewellyn, Clare Oliver, Anna Sandeman
Art editor: Christina Fraser
Illustrations: Chris Forsey pp.4-5, 6-7, 14-15, 20-21, 28-29,
30-31; Nick Harris (Virgil Pomfret Agency) 8-9; Tony Kenyon
(B.L.Kearley Ltd) all cartoons; Nicki Palin 10-11, 18-19;
Maurice Pledger (Bernard Thornton) 16-17, 24-25;
Bryan Poole 12-13, 22-23, 26-27.

CONTENTS

How big is the ocean?

The ocean is truly ENORMOUS! It covers more than twice as much of the Earth as land does. In fact, it's made up of four oceans – the Pacific, the Atlantic, the Indian and the Arctic. Although these all have different names, they flow into each other to make one huge world ocean.

● Don't go for a swim in the Arctic Ocean. It's the coldest of the oceans, and for most of the year it's covered in ice.

Which is the biggest ocean?

The Pacific is by far the biggest ocean in the world. It's larger than the other three oceans put together, and it's also much deeper. If you look at a globe, you'll see that the Pacific reaches halfway around the world.

● These drops of water show the oceans in order of size.

Pacific

What's the difference between a sea and an ocean?

People often use the words sea and ocean to mean the same thing. That's fine, but to a scientist, seas are just part of an ocean – the parts that are nearest to land. The Mediterranean Sea is between Africa and Europe, for example.

Atlantic

Indian

Arctic

Why is the sea salty?

Seawater tastes salty because it has salt in it! The salt is the same as the stuff people sprinkle on food. Most of it comes from rocks on the land. Rain washes the salt into rivers which carry it to the sea.

● Some of the sea salt we use comes from hot places, such as India. People build low walls to trap the seawater when the tide comes in. When the Sun dries up the water, the salt is left behind.

● Most of the Earth's water is salty. Only a tiny part is fresh water that we can drink.

● Some beaches around the Black Sea are covered with rich, dark mud. People slap it all over themselves – it's meant to be good for the skin.

Is the Red Sea really red?

Parts of the Red Sea look red. In summer millions of tiny red plants called algae grow in the water. Don't worry, you won't turn pink if you swim there!

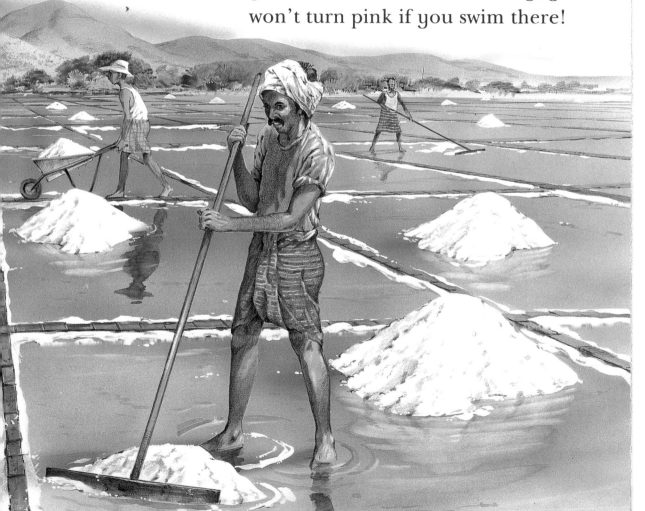

What did sailors fear the most?

In olden days, sailors had to put up with bad food, fearful storms … and pirate attacks! Pirates roamed the high seas, on the look out for merchant ships loaded with fine goods and treasure. When the pirates found a ship they boarded it, attacked the crew, and carried off all the valuable goodies.

● Blackbeard was one of the nastiest pirates. To look extra fierce, he used to thread rope through his beard and then set it on fire!

● Real pirates didn't actually make people walk the plank. But the pirates you read about in stories often do!

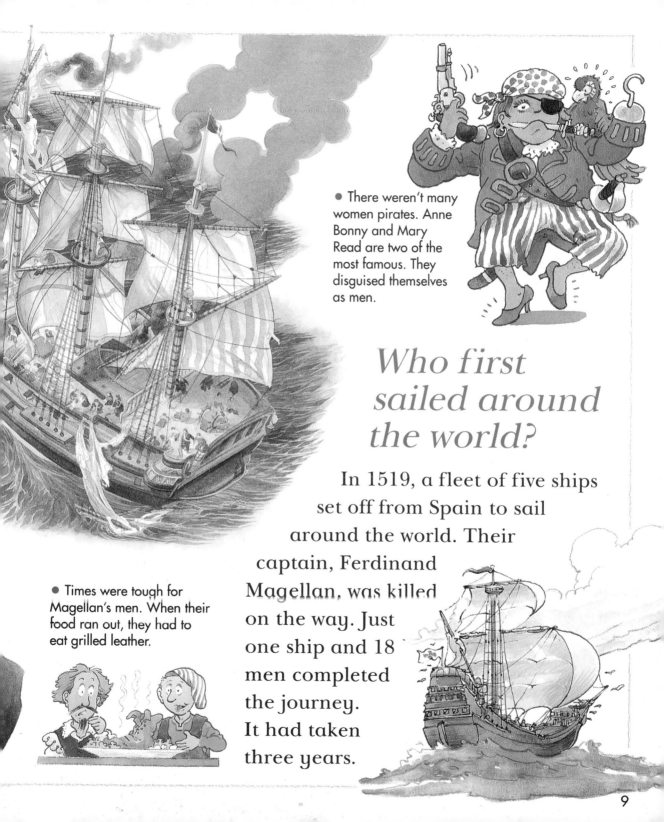

● There weren't many women pirates. Anne Bonny and Mary Read are two of the most famous. They disguised themselves as men.

Who first sailed around the world?

In 1519, a fleet of five ships set off from Spain to sail around the world. Their captain, Ferdinand Magellan, was killed on the way. Just one ship and 18 men completed the journey. It had taken three years.

● Times were tough for Magellan's men. When their food ran out, they had to eat grilled leather.

What is sand made of?

Look closely at a handful of sand, and you'll see that it's made of tiny chips of rock and seashell. The bits of rock come from cliffs that have been broken up by the rain and sea. The shells are washed in by the tide and crushed by the pounding waves.

● Not all sand is yellow. Some beaches have black, pinky-white, or even green sand.

● Hang seaweed outside and it might forecast the weather! If it swells up, rain is on the way. If it dries out, then the Sun will shine.

● Wreckers were people who shone lights to trick ships into crashing on the rocks. Then they stole all the valuable things on board, and hid them in caves.

How are caves made?

As waves hurl sand and rocks against a cliff, it is slowly worn away. The waves scoop out a small hollow, then a deep hole. After a very long time, the hole is worn into a dark, damp and dripping cave.

- A tropical beach may look deserted, but dozens of different plants and animals make their homes there.

- You can often find empty seashells washed up on the beach. Their owners have probably been eaten!

Why do limpets cling to rocks?

Like other animals on the seashore, limpets have a tough life. As the tide comes in, they are battered by the waves. As the tide goes out, they are tugged and pulled about by the swirling water. The poor limpets have to cling tightly to the rocks so that they aren't swept out to sea!

Which fish has headlights?

It's so dark at the bottom of the ocean that some fish make their own light. The angler fish has a long fin dangling in front of its face. At the end of the fin is a blob which glows. Small fish are drawn towards the glowing light, only to disappear into the angler fish's big, gaping mouth.

- The deep sea is inky black and as cold as a fridge. Even so, some amazing creatures live there.

Angler fish

How deep is the ocean?

- The seabed has huge cracks in it, called trenches. Some are over 10 kilometres deep.

Away from the shore, the ocean plunges to about 4 kilometres in most places. That's deep enough to swallow Ben Nevis, Britain's tallest mountain, three times!

Gulper eel

What makes chimneys under the sea?

Fountains of boiling hot water gush out of holes in some parts of the seabed. Tiny grains sink down out of the hot water and build into weird-looking chimney stacks around the holes.

● Many deep-sea fish are real ugly mugs. It's just as well it's so dark down there!

● Giant red-and-white worms as long as buses live around the chimneys.

Dragonfish

What's it like at the bottom of the sea?

You might think that the bottom of the sea is smooth and flat, but it isn't – at least not everywhere. There are mountains and valleys, hills and plains, just as there are on land.

● In 1963, a volcano erupted under the sea near Iceland. Hot, runny rock bubbled up to the surface of the water, and hardened. It made a completely new island, which was named Surtsey.

● Along the shore, the land slopes gently into the sea. This slope is called the continental shelf.

● Flat plains cover half of the sea floor. They are called abyssal plains.

● The Mid-Atlantic Ridge is a long line of underwater mountains in the Atlantic Ocean.

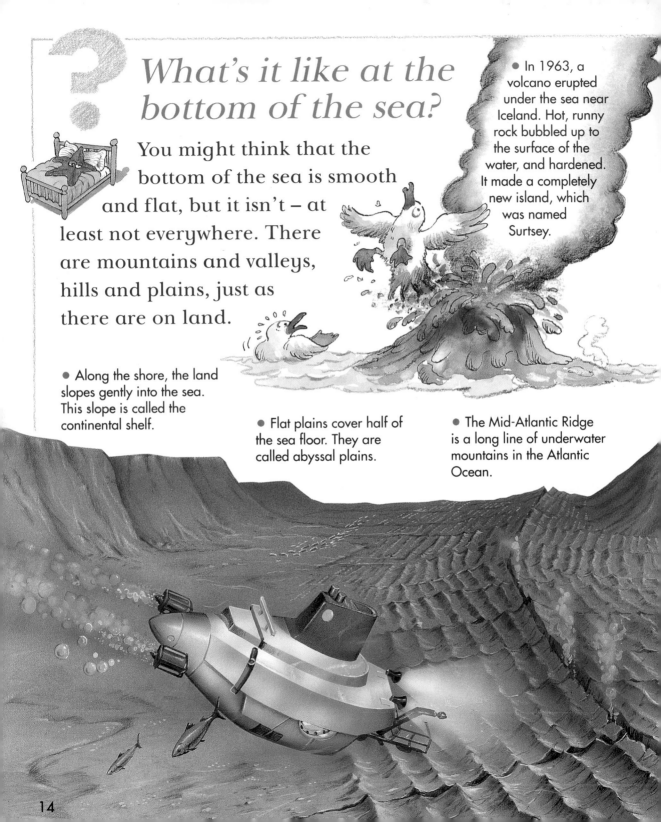

14

Are there mountains under the sea?

Yes, lots – and they are all volcanoes! Someone has counted about 10,000 of them, but there may be double this number. The proper name for them is sea mounts. Some are so high that they stick out of the water and make islands.

● There are earthquakes under the sea, just as there are on land. In fact, there are over a million seaquakes a year! But most of them happen so deep down that we can't feel them.

● A trench is a deep valley in the seabed.

● A sea mount is an underwater volcano. There's a sea mount erupting somewhere as you read this!

How do fish breathe under water?

▷ Not all sea creatures can breathe under water. Sea cows, seals and dolphins breathe air, so they have to keep coming to the surface.

Fish have to breathe to stay alive, just as you do. But while you breathe oxygen from the air, fish take it from water. As they swim, fish gulp in water and push it out through slits called gills on their heads. Oxygen passes from the water into the fish's blood inside their gills.

Gill cover

How do fish swim?

Fish swim by using their muscles to ripple their bodies along. Wiggling their tails from side to side gives them extra push. They use their other fins to balance and change direction.

Which bird flies under water?

Penguins can't fly through the air because their wings are too short and stumpy. They are much more at home in the ocean, where they use their wings as flippers.

● Seahorses aren't strong swimmers. They hang on to seaweed to avoid being swept away.

Which animal is jet-propelled?

Squid don't have flippers or a tail, but they're still fast movers. They suck water into their bodies, then squirt it out so powerfully that their bodies shoot backwards.

● Squid have ten tentacles – that's two more than their relative, the octopus.

Which animal loves to play?

Dolphins are playful and trusting. Some are so friendly they will let you swim with them. Dolphins have even rescued drowning people, by using their noses to nudge them to shore.

How do whales and dolphins use sound to see?

Whales and dolphins use ears, not eyes, to find their way about. As they swim they make clicking noises, which travel through the water. When the clicks hit something solid, an echo bounces back – just like a ball bouncing off a wall. The echo tells the animal what lies ahead.

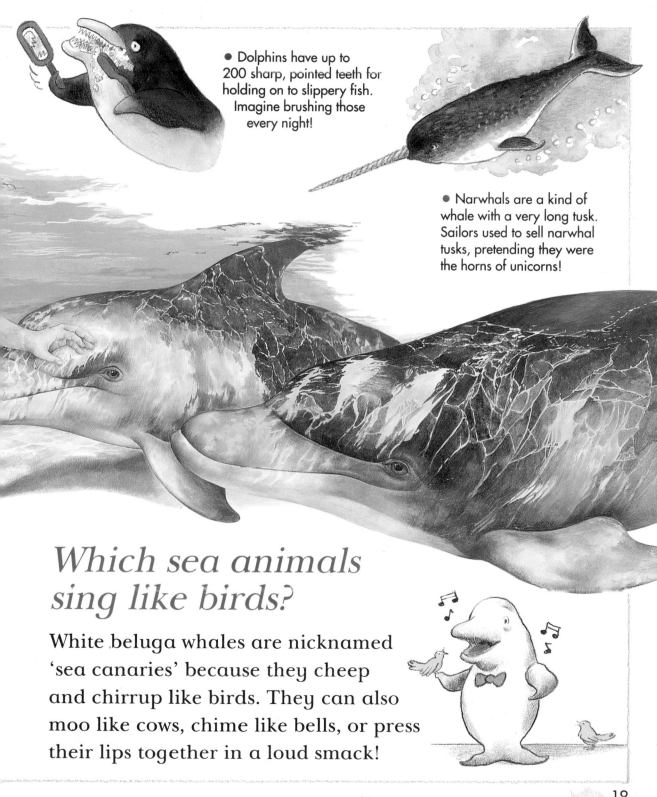

• Dolphins have up to 200 sharp, pointed teeth for holding on to slippery fish. Imagine brushing those every night!

• Narwhals are a kind of whale with a very long tusk. Sailors used to sell narwhal tusks, pretending they were the horns of unicorns!

Which sea animals sing like birds?

White beluga whales are nicknamed 'sea canaries' because they cheep and chirrup like birds. They can also moo like cows, chime like bells, or press their lips together in a loud smack!

What makes waves roll?

Waves are ripples of water blown across the surface of the ocean by the wind. On a calm day they hardly move, but in stormy weather they roll faster and faster, and grow higher and higher, until they form huge walls of water.

● Make your own waves in a bowl of water. The harder you blow across the surface, the bigger the waves.

● Some waves are called white horses because their curly white tips look like horses' manes.

● At Waimea Bay, Hawaii, surfers ride waves up to 10 metres high – that's six times taller than a man!

• Palm trees will grow in a chilly place like Scotland because warm currents flow along the west coast, bringing water from much hotter parts of the world

Are there rivers in the ocean?

The ocean has great bands of water called currents which flow like rivers. They travel faster than the water around them, moving from one part of the world to another.

• Ocean currents can carry a message in a bottle for you. But don't hold your breath. One floated for 73 years before it was washed up!

Why do sailors watch the tides?

Twice a day the sea comes high up the beach, and then goes back again. At high tide the water is deep, and sailing boats can sail in and out of the harbour. But at low tide, the water is so shallow that sailors are either stuck on the shore or out at sea!

• In Canada's Bay of Fundy, the water at high tide is about 15 metres deeper than at low tide – that's the height of a five-storey house!

Where do angels, clowns and parrots live?

Angelfish, clownfish and parrotfish are just some of the thousands of beautiful animals that live on coral reefs. Tropical fish like these often have dazzling colours and bold patterns.

Imperial angelfish

Parrotfish

● Coral reefs grow in shallow water in the warmest parts of the world.

Angelfish

● Giant clams live on coral reefs. Their shells are big enough to have a bath in!

What is a coral reef?

• Corals comes in all sorts of shapes – antlers, plates, mushrooms, feathers, daisies and even brains!

A coral reef is like a beautiful underwater hedge. It looks stony and dead – but it is really alive! Coral is made up of millions of tiny animals, which leave their hard skeletons behind when they die. Each new layer piles on to the old, slowly building the coral rock.

Where is the biggest reef?

The world's biggest coral reef lies in warm shallow seas off the northeast coast of Australia. It's called the Great Barrier Reef, and it stretches for more than 2,000 kilometres. It's so huge that it can be seen by astronauts up in space.

Clown fish

Which is the biggest fish?

The whale shark is the world's biggest fish. It's gigantic – as long as eight scuba divers lying head to toe, and as heavy as six large elephants.

● The dwarf goby is the smallest fish in the ocean.

● The oar fish is the longest fish in the ocean – as long as four canoes placed end to end.

Oar fish

● The biggest sea plant is the giant kelp seaweed. A single strand can grow nearly as long as a football pitch!

Sailfish

Which is the fastest fish?

The sailfish can race along under water at over 100 kilometres an hour – as fast as a car. It tucks its fins in tightly, and its pointed nose cuts through the water like a knife.

Whale shark

Which is the biggest crab?

● The pea-sized pea crab is the smallest crab of all. It lives inside oyster and mussel shells.

Japan's giant spider crab measures nearly 4 metres from the tip of one front claw to the tip of the other. It could open its arms wide enough to hug a hippopotamus!

Which fish hunts with a hammer?

The hammerhead shark has a huge head shaped like a hammer. But this tool is for hunting, not banging in nails. The shark's eyes and nostrils are at each end of the hammer. As the shark swims, it swings its head from side to side, searching for a meal.

● The Portuguese man-of-war catches its tea in its long, stinging tentacles.

Which is the most shocking fish?

Some fish give off electric shocks to protect themselves or to stun animals they want to eat. The most shocking ocean fish is the torpedo ray. If you could switch it on, it would light up a light bulb!

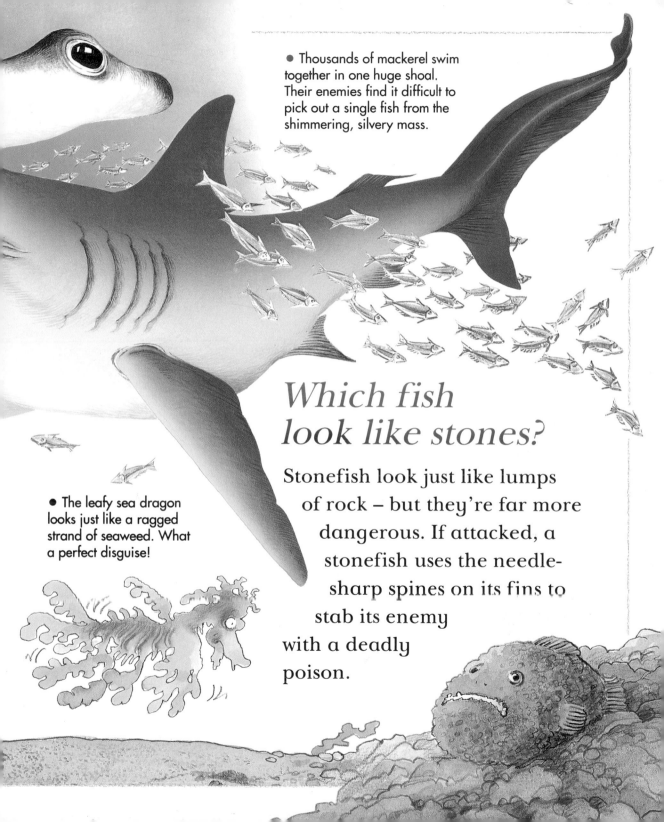

● Thousands of mackerel swim together in one huge shoal. Their enemies find it difficult to pick out a single fish from the shimmering, silvery mass.

Which fish look like stones?

Stonefish look just like lumps of rock – but they're far more dangerous. If attacked, a stonefish uses the needle-sharp spines on its fins to stab its enemy with a deadly poison.

● The leafy sea dragon looks just like a ragged strand of seaweed. What a perfect disguise!

How deep do submarines dive?

Few submarines can dive much lower than 200 metres below the surface of the ocean. That's about 100 times deeper than an Olympic swimming pool.

What dives deepest?

Divers use smaller craft called submersibles to explore deep water and to look for wrecks and sunken treasure. The *Titanic* was an enormous ocean liner which sank over 70 years ago. Divers discovered the wreck 3,781 metres down in 1985. They were able to reach it in a submersible called *Alvin*.

● The *Titanic* was launched in 1912. On its very first voyage, it hit an iceberg and sank in the Atlantic Ocean.

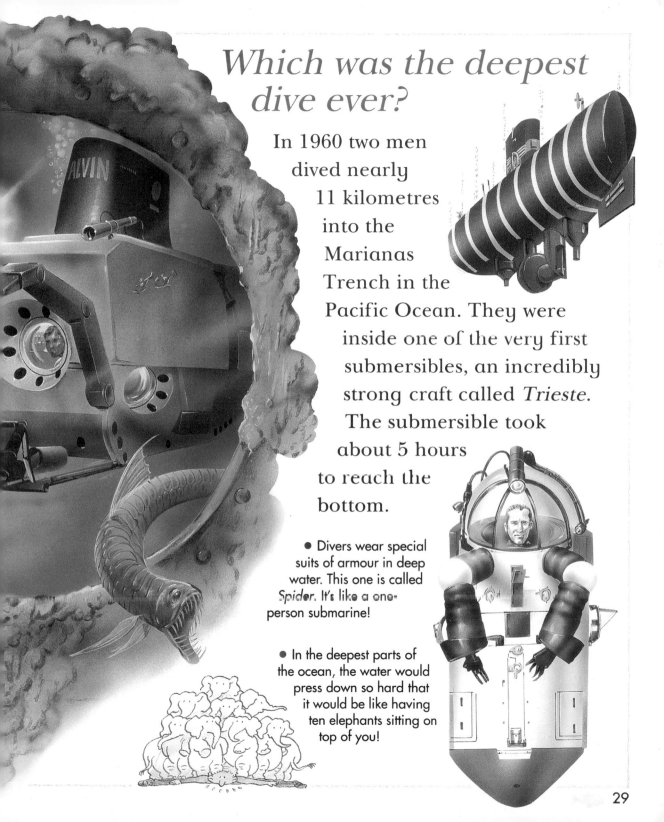

Which was the deepest dive ever?

In 1960 two men dived nearly 11 kilometres into the Marianas Trench in the Pacific Ocean. They were inside one of the very first submersibles, an incredibly strong craft called *Trieste*. The submersible took about 5 hours to reach the bottom.

● Divers wear special suits of armour in deep water. This one is called *Spider*. It's like a one-person submarine!

● In the deepest parts of the ocean, the water would press down so hard that it would be like having ten elephants sitting on top of you!

Who fishes with fire?

On an island in the Pacific Ocean, people fish in the darkness of night. They set fire to the branches of coconut trees, and then hang them over the side of their boats. The fish swim towards the firelight – only to be caught by the islanders' sharp spears.

● Seaweed is rich in goodness, so farmers spread it on their land to improve the soil. It is also used to thicken ice-cream and toothpaste.

Are there farms under the sea?

Yes, but there aren't any farmers, cows or sheep! Some kinds of fish and shellfish are raised in large cages out at sea. The fish are so well fed that they grow much more quickly than they would do in the wild.

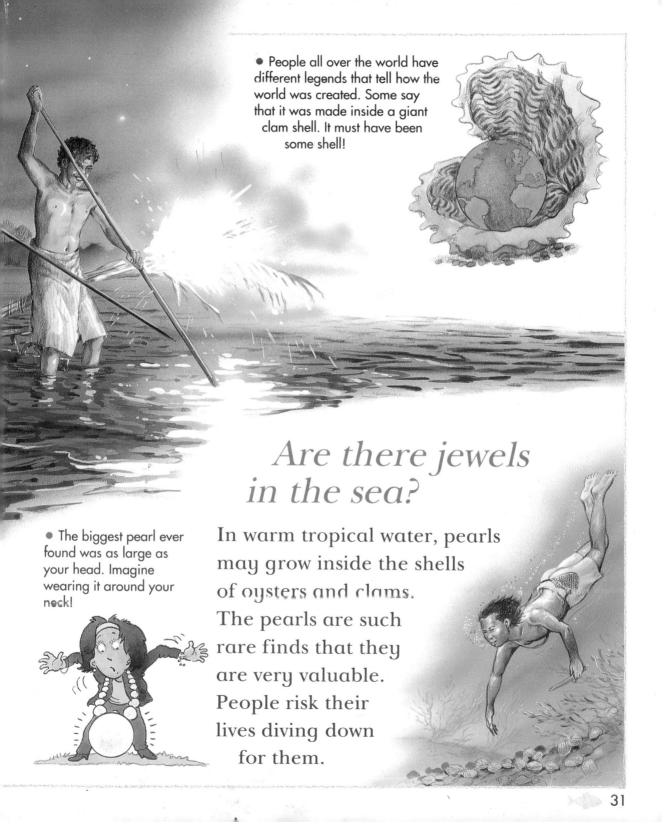

● People all over the world have different legends that tell how the world was created. Some say that it was made inside a giant clam shell. It must have been some shell!

Are there jewels in the sea?

● The biggest pearl ever found was as large as your head. Imagine wearing it around your neck!

In warm tropical water, pearls may grow inside the shells of oysters and clams. The pearls are such rare finds that they are very valuable. People risk their lives diving down for them.

Index

A
abyssal plain 14
Alvin 28
angelfish 22
angler fish 12
Arctic Ocean 4, 5
Atlantic Ocean 4, 5, 14, 28

B
Blackbeard 8

C
cave 10
clam 22, 31
clownfish 22
continental shelf 14
coral reef 22-23
crab 25
current, ocean 21

D
diving 28-29
dolphin 16, 18, 19

F
fish 12, 13, 16, 22, 24, 26, 27, 30
fishing 30

G
gills 16
Great Barrier Reef 23

I
Indian Ocean 4, 5

L
limpet 11

M
Magellan, Ferdinand 9
Mediterranean Sea 5
Mid-Atlantic Ridge 14

N
narwhal 19

O
oar fish 24

P
Pacific Ocean 4, 5, 29, 30, 31
parrotfish 22
penguin 17
pirate 8-9

R
Red Sea 7

S
sailfish 24
salt 6
sand 10
seahorse 17
sea mount 15
seashell 10, 11, 25, 31
seaweed 10, 24, 30
shark 24, 26
squid 17
stonefish 27
submarine 28
submersible 28, 29

T
tide 10, 11, 21
torpedo ray 26
Trieste 29

V
volcano, underwater 14, 15

W
wave 10, 11, 20
whale 18, 19
wrecker 10